Don't Do What We Did!
A Conversation About Online Dating With an Ex-Not-Quite-Couple Who Met on the Internet

ISBN 978-1466308800

Cover design: ManjariGraphics

Cover illustration: Corne Cartoons – Enroc Illustrations CO

Michelle's photo: Eric Johnson-Gamez, Visual Concepts Photography

Ricardo's photo: Sandy Kolar

Editor: Sharon Honeycutt

Hearts and minds and technology intertwine to become one.

~ Michelle Y. Talbert

Dedicated to hopeful romantics everywhere.

~ Michelle

Dedicated to the possibility of finding true love…or not.

~Ricardo

Table of Contents

Introduction

"Nice smile." That message, sent from one online dating account to another, began a whirlwind love affair and subsequent friendship between Ricardo and Michelle that led us to write this book.

Welcome! If you're like us, you're single (or some semblance thereof) and have either contemplated online dating, have dipped a toe into the waters of the online-dating scene, or have jumped right into the water off of the diving board. Unfortunately, for all of your efforts, you still haven't found that person you're seeking. Well, neither have we. But, what we have found is each other. And through trial and error in our relationship with one another, through experiences that friends and loved ones have shared with us, and through the relationships we've had with others in the twenty-plus years we've collectively spent looking for love in technological places, we believe we've amassed a great deal of information about what works and, more importantly, what doesn't work when dating online.

Between us we have had four marriages, three and one-half divorces (Michelle has been separated for two years), some kids, cats and dogs, various romantic relationships, heartbreaks, great sex, and not-so-great sex. Through all of this, we're both still pretty happy and well-adjusted people, even though we're still single.

According to dating site commercials, 20 percent of relationships now begin online. Even if that number is inflated, it's a fact that with varying degrees of "success" more and more people are meeting online. Once we (Ricardo and Michelle) determined that we probably weren't a love connection, we began comparing notes about some of the experiences we had had prior to and since meeting each other. Ironically, we are both back on the website where we met! We have reconciled, for the most part, what went wrong between us (hey, we're human) and, during that process, discussed some of the pitfalls and positive attributes of relationships that begin online. We realize that even though more and more people are meeting online, there are still a large number who are not getting the results they want. That's where we come in. This book represents our promise to each other and to you to be honest and to share our insight about online dating—the good, the bad, and the ugly.

Michelle talks to the fellas out there about how they can improve their online skills and attract the type of woman they're pursuing, without harming all the women they meet along the path to The One. Ricardo hopes to decode the behaviors exhibited by many of the men online and give women a peek into their minds. As he says, "I think all men want to be good, but we kind of start off being bad." He also shares some Man Code—yeah, he knows his boys may not be speaking to him by the end of this book—but ladies, he's willing to risk it for you!

We discuss the do's and don'ts of profiles, pictures, electronic and telephonic communications, and, of course, the all-important, first face-to-face meeting—or not. Some people seek only pen pals. We share with you some mistakes we made. For example, Michelle got into Ricardo's car the first night we met. Even though we were only driving two blocks, this was a serious safety issue. By the way, that first message was sent by Ricardo, but she 'initiated' first contact, we'll discuss how. These anecdotes, served up with a good helping of humor, will let you know that you're not alone in your quest. Even if you don't meet the love of your life online, hopefully you'll meet a really cool person or two—like we did—who you can call 'friend'—with or without benefits. Our sincere hope is that our honesty, for better or for worse, will improve your chances for success online.

We are honored and excited to share our story with you, as a cautionary tale of sorts and a story of what amazing things can happen when we remain open to the possibilities that life brings our way. It is our sincere hope that the wisdom we've gained from the crystal clear, 20/20 vision of hindsight will help you along your journey to find who you are searching for online. We're not perfect, but we're perfectly qualified to tell you what not to do!

Michelle & Ricardo
Washington, DC
August 2011

Chapter 1 Love, Lust & Loneliness

Michelle:	Ricardo, why are you writing this book?
Ricardo:	Well, I've always been intrigued by this online dating thing. I've been online for probably seven years, and when you suggested that you wanted to get together and write a book about it, I was very interested in doing it because I'd like to give women an inside track as to what we men think about, why we do the things we do, and why we say the things we say. I guess I'd like to make it easier for women to find a good man online.
	Also, this book is going to be a learning tool for me because you're also telling *me* what women think. So, I'm letting you know what men think, and I'm also learning. I'm getting the woman's perspective, too.
Michelle:	You said that you wanted to help women find good men online. Are there any good men online?
Ricardo:	There are some good men online. I think all men want to be good, but we kind of start off being bad.
Ricardo:	Michelle, it's your turn. Why are you writing this book?
Michelle:	Since I've been single again, the topic of dating online has come up in conversations with my friends, and it's

now prevalent in the media. It seemed to me, though, that so many of us are just out there flailing about without any real guidance. While there are some success stories, most of the people I know are really not finding what they thought they could find online, at least not as far as long-term relationships. So, when you and I dated and shared some of our own stories as well as our friends' stories with each other, I noticed some similarities, but I also had a few epiphanies. I thought, "Wow! Wouldn't it be great if each of us could know a little about what our love interest thinks?" You and I are so comfortable talking to each other that I thought it could be fun and enlightening for others if we had this conversation openly. With any luck, we will all walk away having learned something helpful that we didn't know before.

Excuse me, What is My Motivation?

Michelle: What do you think drives men to go to an online site in the first place?

Ricardo: In my case, I went online for the first time to try something new. It was probably—shoot—seven or so years ago.

Michelle: So when you say you wanted to try something new, does that mean you wanted to meet someone to hang out with, or ...?

Ricardo: Yeah. I just wanted a new way to meet people. It was something different.

Actually, I have a cousin who pretty much introduced me to online dating, and, once I got on there, I saw how easy it was to get women. It's like going to the club, but you're sitting in front of your computer. It's a lot less effort.

Michelle: So, is it about finding sex, or is it for finding a relationship?

Ricardo: Well, for me at first, yeah, it was just sex.

Michelle: But that was seven years ago. What is it now?

Ricardo: Now it's sex.

Michelle: It's always sex, right?

Ricardo: Yeah, pretty much. Actually, for most men it may be sex at the outset, but I think everyone is online with the long-term goal of finding someone. No one wants to grow old alone. But I don't know. Online dating is fun. I like talking and interacting with people, chatting, going back and forth.

Michelle: Yeah, there is a bit of an adrenaline rush when you are first getting to know someone—maybe because the possibilities of a new relationship are exciting? Many men say that they're looking for relationships or are open to the possibilities of relationships. Are you saying that this is untrue, or are some men more open than others? I've talked to more than one woman who has told me that she began an online relationship with a man who said he also wanted a

relationship only to discover—in the
end—that wasn't true.

For example, one friend of ours went online to find a
relationship. She had never really been online before, and she went
on one date with a man who appeared to be exactly what she was
looking for. He said that he wanted a relationship, and she was
over the moon. It's now twelve months later, and she is the mother
of a beautiful, precious bundle of love, but the guy she met is gone.
The blessing is that she's still over the moon because she has her
first child, and she loves her dearly. But she was involved with
someone who really wasn't looking for a long-term relationship
even though he said he was.

Ricardo: Some guys just aren't looking for long-
                              term relationships. A friend of mine asked
                              me about a site that I'm on because he was
                              going to Philly for the weekend and
                              wanted to set up a page to see if he could
                              find a woman to keep him company for
                              the weekend.

What we found is that this isn't uncommon. We
interviewed a few guys who have set up "temporary" profiles for
the purpose of finding companionship in geographic locations
away from where they live—from a few hundred miles to a few
thousand miles away. Many of these men stated that they had
traveled for various reasons and that meeting women was not the
purpose for their trips—it was secondary. However, a few
mentioned that they traveled to distant locales because they'd met
someone online and were curious enough to travel the distance to
spend time with the woman. One guy mentioned that while he set
up the profile intending to have only weekend or temporary
companionship, he ended up having two long-distance
relationships that stemmed from what was to be a weekend tryst.

Additionally, when we pushed the men to reveal whether
they make the women aware that they don't live in the area and are

just visiting, the men said "it depends." Michelle raised an eyebrow at these responses. Ricardo, however, nodded in understanding.

Ricardo:

This goes back to men telling women what men think the women want to hear so that the men can get to the next level. At some point, the women will be told the truth, but, instead of saying everything at the beginning or in their profile, some men wait to feel out the woman when they speak or meet. But remember, Michelle, it can still lead to a relationship. I really think men are more open to just going with the flow than women.

One woman we spoke with mentioned that she met a man online, and, when they spoke for the first time, he was packing for a business trip to South America. He told her that he would like for her to come over and give him some "happy travels" sex. She declined. To his credit, she had no doubts about his intentions from the outset!

Networking

Michelle:

It's interesting to me that there are people who use dating sites to further their business aspirations. They make dating sites a part of their marketing strategy— for networking and to sell services and goods. I've been contacted for travel discounts, personal training, and real estate investment opportunities.

Ricardo:

Oh yeah, this lady sends me these invitations to mingle at local dating get-togethers. I've never attended. She and I have never really communicated otherwise and have never met in person. That's all she does is organize these events and send invites. Sometimes people are scamming too, but we'll talk about that in the safety chapter.

People do go online for various reasons. Some are looking for short-term interaction, others for long-term, and still others are seeking business opportunities. It's funny, we both had romantic reasons for going online, and we ended up collaborating on this book!

Up next, we're going to talk about your 'calling card'—otherwise known as your profile. This is where you introduce yourself and articulate your desires to a universe of people—one of whom just might meet those desires.

Chapter 2 You only get one chance to make a first impression: Profile Matters

Your dating profile is your initial presentation to the other members of the dating community. It's how people get to know a little bit about you—just enough that they will want to contact you so that they can get to know more. It's important that you put your best foot forward here so that hopefully you'll capture the attention of the people who have the potential to be the best match for you and to provide the type of relationship you're looking for.

A picture is worth a thousand words

Michelle: Do you think that online dating makes people shallow? We really do place a high level of importance on someone's profile and on the profile picture when we think about initiating contact.

Ricardo: Not necessarily. I think that when you first get online you may be like that but, for men, we don't have as many options as women. I mean, it seems that there are so many more men online than women. Most of the women I know get hundreds of messages from men and men get so much less interest. It seems like online women have the upper hand and can choose whomever, so for men, we feel like we're competing with so many other men for the attention of the women we're interested in.

Michelle: Wow, that's interesting. In traditional dating it feels like, and numerically is the reality, that men have the upper hand and women are competing for a shrinking pool of men.

We asked one of our male interviewees about online dating and using pictures as the basis for deciding whether or not you move forward with a person's profile. He answered this way:

I think that online dating can actually make you less shallow because before you even initiate contact, you have more information about a person than you would have if you met in a club or out somewhere. Most of the time, I know whether a woman has kids or if she smokes. So, while it may begin with the picture, I have a depth of knowledge about her before we even say hello. So, no, I definitely think it doesn't make you shallow because you start with a picture. All interaction begins with whether you're physically attracted to the person.

Michelle: I admit that I've bypassed men whose profiles weren't physically attractive to me. Then they've messaged me and said something witty or something that made me realize that they may be a nice guy.

Ricardo: Exactly. It can start shallow, but you find that when someone has a personality you like, you're open to seeing where it may lead.

All right, so what attracts you to a person's profile? Guys want to know what to do, how to set up their profile, what to say, and what type of picture to have up there that will attract the most women.

Michelle: The most?

Ricardo: Yeah.

Michelle: So it's about quantity, not quality?

Ricardo: It's about quantity, and then quality can come after that.

Michelle: I would say put up your best picture as your profile picture. And when I say, "best picture," I mean the one that shows who you are *today*, not fifteen years ago, not back when you were in the military …

Ricardo: … or, high school.

Michelle: … or in high school, or in college when you were shooting hoops because now you weigh 300 pounds. Be truthful in that first profile pic. I don't know that that's going to get you *the most* women, but at least it will attract women who are attracted to you.

Ricardo: So do you like guys to smile in their pictures?

Michelle: Oh yeah. I think so. But not necessarily.

Ricardo: Wear a suit?

Michelle: Not necessarily because you know women are just as varied in what we are attracted to as men. It depends on the type of woman you're trying to attract. I'm a professional woman; however, I like guys who wear casual clothing. Most of the women who I've spoken with or most of the women in my circle are also

9

professional women, but that doesn't mean that every picture in a man's profile has to show him in a suit. No matter what he's wearing, he should look well kept in terms of cleanliness and ...

Ricardo: Clean, clean cut.

Michelle: No, not clean cut. No, because loads of brothers with dread locks look great. So, the bottom line is just look attractive, and that's all subjective. We all find different things attractive, but I would say that being honest through your pictures is really the key. Even though you might meet a whole lot of women putting up your high school picture, when they meet you face-to-face, they're going to be pissed off. I've had that happen to me.

Ricardo: So what did you do when it happened?

Michelle: I was nice.

Ricardo: You were "nice"?

Michelle: Yeah. What else are you going to do?

Ricardo: It's happened to me, and I was nice.

Michelle: My brother, I'm going to call you out on that one.

Ricardo: I mean, I was nice to a certain extent.

Michelle: Let's talk a little bit about you and me. You and I met online, and we met in person just a week later. We hadn't had a whole lot of interaction online, and we decided that we were going to meet after I got out of Zumba at the gym, which is crazy. I would not suggest you meet somebody when you're sweaty.

Ricardo: Why not? That's a good thing. At least I knew that when you said in your profile that you worked out and loved Zumba, it was true.

Michelle: Well, we met in the lobby of the gym, and it was a little nerve-wracking for me because I was sweaty. Nonetheless, I came out to say a quick hello and then went to the locker room to clean up a little and get my things. But, I recall asking you what you would have done if I hadn't looked like my picture. Do you remember what you told me?

Ricardo: I would have left.

Michelle: Exactly! You would have left while I was getting my stuff out of my locker. So wrong. So wrong.

Ricardo: But no, I've met people that didn't look like their pictures.

Michelle: What did you do?

Ricardo: They never saw me again.

Michelle: Why is that?

Ricardo: Because I feel like, "You did not represent yourself truthfully."

Michelle: So, you feel they lie?

Ricardo: Yes. They misrepresented themselves to me.

Michelle: OK, so pictures should be recent and accurately represent what you currently look like. If you do put up pictures of yourself in your heyday—which is fine— let it be known that that's what they are.

Ricardo: I agree. Maybe say something like, "This is back in the day, and now I look different. Maybe you can help me get back to how I used to look." Especially if it's related to body size.

Michelle: Right. Perfect. Perfect. Because there are all kinds of people online, and people have all types of attractions. I also have one more thought about pictures, while we're on the subject—know when to stop.

Ricardo: Don't put too many pictures up. I don't even want to look at all those pictures. When I see women with a lot of pictures, I'm thinking, "OK, this person is self-absorbed, and she just loves herself too much. Why do you have a whole album on the site?"

Michelle: Right. It's not Facebook. Whittle them down to a few pictures in different situations. But it's not just women who do this. I've seen sixty or more pictures of a guy in an album. That's bananas.

Ricardo: He's not going to have time to talk to you because he's going to be too busy checking himself out in the mirror.

Michelle: Exactly, I think that men should just put up pictures that show themselves in as natural a pose as possible, just being themselves.

Now, what is it that would help a woman attract the type of man she's looking for? See, you all might want quantity, but I would have to say that we women want quality. So what kind of pictures should we post to put our best foot forward to attract the kind of man we want?

Ricardo: Every guy I've spoken with—and I agree—says that we need to see the face, but then we also need to see the whole body. A lot of times, a woman will just put up pictures of her face, and then in the heading it'll say she has a few extra pounds or whatever. That leaves us guys thinking, "What the hell is that?" A few? That could mean anything in terms of her body type.

Michelle: But those are the categories and options that the sites provide, right? You have to check a box, and the options are kind of generic stuff regarding body type.

Ricardo: Yeah, yeah. Those are the options that you have, but my thing is, put a picture up there. You can put one of your face smiling or whatever and a full body shot so that we can get a view of the whole you. I don't want to see a whole bunch of pictures of just your face.

Michelle: What does that make you think if you just see the face?

Ricardo: That she's a big girl.

Michelle: Is there anything wrong with that?

Ricardo: There's nothing wrong with that. Some people are looking for big girls, but that's not my type. I mean, if you're just putting pictures of your face up there, that tells me that you're ashamed of your body or that you feel like you have something to hide. Show me the whole body so that I can make a choice and not end up meeting you and being like, "Damn."

Michelle: Is this coming from experience?

Ricardo: Yeah, it's happened. It's happened to me, and I have plenty of friends who it's happened to also. They can be as pretty as they want to be, but if I'm not expecting her to be a bigger girl, then I'm blindsided when we meet. So, just get all of that out of the way and avoid any confusion. Plus, if you put up a full body pic and you are larger, then men who are interested in larger women will notice you, and everyone will be happy. But, the really big thing that a lot of guys tell me is that women shouldn't put pictures of their kids on their site.

Michelle: I believe women feel the same way. Although there are some women who may think, "What a great father," I think that the majority would agree that it's

14

inappropriate to put pictures of your children on your profile.

Ricardo: My thing is why? What are you trying to show by putting pictures of your children up?

Michelle: My problem with it is that there are freaks online. I'm not willing to expose my children.

Ricardo: I agree, you shouldn't do that. It's crazy to me that women would put pictures of their babies out there and that a dude would see the picture of the kid and want to hang out with the woman and her baby in the beginning. I don't like that at all, and I know a lot of guys who say, "I don't know why she has pictures of her kids up there." Especially as a father, I just really don't think that pictures of your children should be on your profile at all.

Michelle: I just thought of something else that I forgot to mention—men putting up pictures that have their ex-girlfriends or ex-wives in them because they think those are the only pictures they look good in.

Ricardo: Oh no.

Michelle: I've seen pictures where there's a man and a woman in the picture, and, if you don't know the relationship between them, you're left questioning, "Why is he putting up a picture of himself with a woman on his profile?" I've also seen pictures where men have tried to crop a woman out of the picture. There might be a woman sitting on a man's lap, and he tried to crop around her. Some men will just scratch out the woman's face and leave the rest of her body in the picture—hair and all. I think, "What is that?" I guess those men just really aren't putting too much effort into their profiles.

Ricardo: Yeah, that's tacky.

Michelle: I think that's really a turnoff for women. I see a lot of men do that. I don't know if they just don't have that many pictures of themselves alone, but, shoot, everybody has a camera phone at this point. Take a picture in the bathroom. Put it up and be by yourself in your photo.

Ricardo: In the bathroom? Ewww, Michelle, I don't like bathroom pictures.

Michelle: Actually, a lot of women say the same thing, but people like to take pictures in a mirror, so … bathroom it is.

Ricardo: Well, I say no bathroom pictures and no blurry pictures and DEFINITELY don't have stuff lying around in the background.

Michelle: Talk about that a little bit. Have you seen many pictures where women don't clean the room in the background? Do you make any judgments if you see a woman with a messy background?

Ricardo: Oh, hell yeah. I've seen pictures with the room really messy, with stuff laying everywhere and clothes all over the place.

I think, "She's trifling." All guys think the same way.

Michelle: I heard that there was some kind of study. It was probably a *Cosmo* survey where they asked men, "Would you rather have amazing sex in a messy bedroom or mediocre sex in a clean bedroom?" What do you think most men chose?

Ricardo: Mediocre sex in a clean bedroom.

Michelle: Absolutely. Absolutely. So, men make a lot of judgments. Even though they're apparently only looking at you for sex in the beginning, if your house looks messy, that would decrease the number of men who might reach out to you.

Ricardo: Yeah, it will decrease the chance of her getting contacted, but I'll be honest and say that if she's really attractive, then her attractiveness may outweigh my negative judgments about her messy background.

Michelle: OK.

Ricardo: I know another thing that I don't really like is when I see women who have pictures of their house. They do that.

Michelle: Like the outside of the house?

Ricardo: Yeah, like the caption reads, "My house."

Michelle: What?

Ricardo: Or, "My car," and all that.

Michelle:	Really? Are they usually fancy or something?
Ricardo:	Yeah, yeah. I mean, they might be pictures of a nice house or whatever, but not necessarily.
Michelle:	I'm trying to think. I've seen men take pictures of themselves in front of their cars or on their motorcycles.
Ricardo:	Do you think that's kind of corny?
Michelle:	I think it's extremely corny. I actually don't reach out to men who do that.
Ricardo:	Yeah, my man just set his profile up, and he has a picture of his motorcycle sitting there, and then it's like his Mercedes-Benz is in the background.
Michelle:	Wow, it seems like he's trying too hard.
Ricardo:	I told him. I said, "Come on, man, what message are you trying to send?" I told him not to do it, but he felt that those were the pictures he wanted to put up.
Michelle:	What is someone trying to prove by putting their material possessions in their profile pictures?
Ricardo:	I guess flaunting your possessions works for some people.
Michelle:	I was going to ask you about that because again, when setting up your profile, it always has to go back to who are you trying to hook, right?

Ricardo:	Right. If you're looking for a guy that's going to be materialistic, go ahead and put your house up there. Then, when he just wants you for your money, you can't be surprised. You know one thing I liked about you?
Michelle:	Hmm?
Ricardo:	Is that you didn't put your business out there. You put something totally off in your profession. You said you were a writer. I didn't find out you were a lawyer until we met. I liked that. It's like you weren't trying to be, "Hey, I'm this, and I'm that," and I liked that. We like honesty.
Michelle:	Oh, but you all aren't honest. You know we're going to keep revisiting this.
Ricardo:	Yeah. We like honesty. We like honesty, but it's hard to come by though.

A picture may open the door to getting your profile read, but, for the most part, what you write about yourself in your profile is what will help your prospect decide whether to move forward or move on. Unless you have an attractive physique, or as Ricardo says, "If she has a phat ass, then it really won't matter what's in her profile," because he's going to, "at least say 'hi.'"

Who are you?

Michelle:	Okay, so we've talked about pictures. Now, in terms of the actual profile itself,

are there things that you've seen that are red flags? Have you read things that are a turn-on or that will draw you to a person?

Ricardo: Well, as far as I'm concerned—and a lot of men are concerned—we're kind of primitive.

Michelle: You mean you're visual? So, it's more so about the picture than the words?

Ricardo: Yeah, exactly. If I see a long profile, I usually don't read it. I will skim through it and pick out the little parts that I kind of want to read. But for me and a lot of the guys I've spoken with, we all agree that the profile should be quick and to the point. Women should be precise with what they want and just say it. I mean, you can tell me what you're like, but you don't have to write a book—no pun intended. Don't make it too long. What in a man's profile do women look at?

Michelle: When you were saying that men don't read long profiles, I chuckled because actually the lead in to my current profile is, "You all don't read this anyway, do you?" You'd be surprised how many messages I've received that say, "Yes, we do read them. We read profiles." Now, of course, they could just be reading the first line and then saying that to try to get in good with me...

Ricardo: Pretty much. Men are smart. We're smart enough to know what to say and what to do.

20

Michelle: To get in the door?

Ricardo: Yeah.

One of the women who shared her story of online dating with us pointed out that she realized that she met so many men who appeared to be the man of her dreams because she laid out all that was important to her and all that she was looking for in her profile. When people write too much in their profiles, they open the door for people to present exactly what is stated in the profile. It's unfortunate to think that there are people who would prey upon us and use that type of information to harm us, but in online dating, sometimes less is more. Let information unfold over time. We think that we're ensuring that we'll get people to respond who are what we are looking for. Sometimes, though, we get people who present what we're looking for. There's a difference.

Michelle: I've seen a lot of profiles where men say things to tap into different parts of a woman. I've seen profiles that say, "I'm new to the area." If you're looking for a woman who's a caretaker, you're going to find a woman who reaches out to you and says, "I'd love to show you around. Oh, there's great things to see in DC."

Ricardo: I need to put that in my profile.

Michelle: I bet you do. And then there are the profiles that say, "I've never done this before. This is new to me." This gives women a (false) sense of comfort that he's not one of those long-time, user/predator kind of dudes. For me, having had the experience of being off and online for so many years, those are red flags. But I would think for women who haven't had as much experience online, or who aren't aware, or who haven't read our book yet, that they would be drawn in by these comments because they tap into that mother instinct that a lot of us have because we want to take care of you guys. Something that helps me know that a guy is real is if he says, "I'm not trying to rush things." But that may be a line.

Ricardo: Yeah, it is pretty much.

Michelle: But, I guess only time can tell, but if I really don't rush things then either he'll stick around or he won't.

One of the men we interviewed mentioned that he rotates around different sites, and he comes off of sites for extended periods of time then goes back on. He does this because over time your profile becomes stale and people—especially women—wonder how you could be online for such long periods of time, especially if a man says that he's looking for a relationship. Ricardo closed his online account the week after he and Michelle met, and she closed hers shortly thereafter. We'll discuss closing accounts in a later chapter, but know that there are various reasons for closing accounts.

Who do you hope to meet? Are you sure?

Michelle: Okay, so some guys play games to make women trust them more?

Ricardo: No, not all guys do that.

Michelle: Tell me about the guys that don't do that. Let's talk about the good guys.

Ricardo: In my profile I don't say anything about, "I'm new to the area. Please show me this or whatever." I'm not doing any of that.

Michelle:	If I recall correctly, though, your tagline is, "Just trying this out," which kind of implies this is new to you, doesn't it?
Ricardo:	That's true. That's true. So now I'm getting women who want to show me the ropes.
Michelle:	Exactly.
Ricardo:	Well that's good. That's a good thing.
Michelle:	Do you mean that's good for you because you like nurturing women?
Ricardo:	But that's still not me saying I'm new to the area.
Michelle:	No, you're not saying you're new to the area, but you're saying you're new to something.
Ricardo:	So maybe subconsciously I *am* trying to attract the nurturing women. I don't know.
Michelle:	So I think that in terms of trying to attract the type of person you're interested in, you need to clearly identify your purposes for being online in your profile. I'm still going to take issue with you, though. I do not believe that all men on there are seeking sex.
Ricardo:	I don't say, "Just trying this out." I say, "Just checking it out."
Michelle:	Ugh, it's the same thing. OK, Ricardo? Nonetheless, it's possible that based on your tagline or certain words that you use, you can attract a certain type of woman. I

don't know whether or not you guys do this consciously or subconsciously but …

Ricardo: I think it's subconsciously. I think our personalities—whatever our personalities may be—we kind of exude it in our profiles.

Michelle: Okay, so let's talk a little bit about that. We talked about what you may do subconsciously in your profile. What about the conscious choices you make? What are some of the things that you find that women highlight that draw you to them or that make you want to ask more questions? We know that you guys are visual, so once you've decided you're physically attracted to her, what do you look at?

Ricardo: I look at whether she smokes, or if she drinks socially—general things that are check-the-box options. I determine whether those attributes are in line with my own and then decide whether to reach out.

Michelle: We talked a little bit earlier about what it means to be a 'few extra pounds.' You only have a certain number of categories you can click when it comes to body type, but I find that women—and tell me if this is inaccurate—we tend to view our bodies a bit more negatively than men view theirs. Case in point, I know that there have been times when I may have clicked—I don't know—big-boned, or whatever the options are, and …

Ricardo:	BBW.
Michelle:	Right.
Ricardo:	What the hell is that? Big and beautiful?
Michelle:	Big, beautiful women, I think. If someone meets me, they say, "You're not that. Why would you click that?" But I find that a lot of men tend to go in the opposite direction, and a lot of them tend to click 'athletic' when they look like sumo wrestlers. Sumo wrestlers may be athletes to some, but they are not the kind of athlete I'm looking for.
Ricardo:	Just to you, though, but somebody else might say, "Oh he's athletic."
Michelle:	Yeah. Like Refrigerator Perry is athletic, right?
Ricardo:	Or, women look at me, and I say I'm athletic, and they look at me and say, "Oh wow ..."
Michelle:	"You're skinny."
Ricardo:	"You're skinny. You're a skinny guy."
Michelle:	Until you take off your shirt. And they see you cut up like a bag of dope?
Ricardo:	You heard?
Michelle:	Are there things that women can put in their profile that you think will help them draw quality men?
Ricardo:	Well, the first thing is put a full body picture in there.

Michelle: Words. Words, Ricardo. Are you saying that words don't matter?

Ricardo: As far as words that they can put in their profile? Be honest and brief.

Michelle: So are you and I—through this book—going to start a crusade for honesty in profiles for both men and women because, if so, you need to talk to your brothers a little bit about the honesty thing.

Ricardo: I think so, yeah. We men do need to be a little more forthcoming about ourselves, but you can't tell everything. Like, if you say, "Okay, well I was locked up three times but I'm not a child molester or anything like that. I'm just a criminal, but I've changed my life around…"

Michelle: That's a little too much. See, I don't want to know that. Well, maybe I do.

Safety is a big concern. In a later chapter, we'll discuss things that people can do to protect themselves.

Ricardo: And you know what I really look at? 'Some college,' 'Master's degree,' 'Ph.D.' Ph.D. is a turn on. She can look like Shrek, but if she has a Ph.D., I'm going to at least say 'Hi.'

Michelle: Well, maybe not Shrek, but Fiona, huh?

Ricardo: No, I'm not that shallow.

Michelle: No. You are the man who likes sex with smart women, right?

Ricardo: I love smart women. Most men do.

Michelle: Even if the men are dumb as a box of rocks, huh?

Ricardo: All of the men that I have talked to have said that's the thing that—aside from pictures—draws them in. Look at me, I have a high school education, a little bit—teeny, little teeny bit of college—but I love smart women.

Michelle: So, in terms of things that women can say about themselves, we should pretty much just be honest.

Ricardo: Just be honest.

Michelle: Don't tell too much information.

Ricardo: And, please, please don't be too negative in your profile. A lot of women say things like, "Don't waste my time," "Don't play games with me," "Please read my entire profile before you message me with boring questions that are answered in my profile." I read these kinds of profiles and sit there and think, "Wow, is she bitter? What happened to her to make her so hostile before someone even contacts her?" Honestly, when most men see profiles like that, it doesn't matter how pretty or smart or attractive the woman is, we know that she's going to be negative, so we just keep it moving.

Michelle: Yes, underlying pain and anger can come out in a profile. Men do it too. I've read profiles where men have a list of "Don't contact me if ..." One guy's profile said, "Don't contact me if you're over thirty and you still wear Hello Kitty clothing." I was personally offended because I have the cutest Hello Kitty t-shirt! I really do believe that in some ways you can feel underlying anger or other issues if you're reading between the lines. Sometimes it's not even about what they say, it's about what's left unsaid. I recall one time that a guy responded to one of my profiles where I mentioned how it just happens to work out that I date younger men. I had this man go at me in so many messages about how I was missing out on real guys, and when my young dude chose his Xbox over me, I'd find out all there was to know about being with a younger man. I mean, he was really personally affronted that I like younger men. He was about fifty years old.

Ricardo:

He was attacking you.

Michelle:

He was attacking me when I didn't even say anything negative. I didn't say that I don't like older men. I just listed my personal preference for younger men.

Ricardo:

Who does that, though? The guys in my circle wouldn't reach out to a woman to scream on her because she stated that she had a preference that didn't match their characteristics.

Michelle:

You and I have talked about race. We both happen to have an affinity for people of our same race. At one point, I recall you saying you had something in your profile about that. I've seen men with profiles that say, "All races welcome." Did you ever have any negative consequence because you say, "I love my sisters"? OK, Black Man, talk a little bit about being a black man who loves your sisters and the consequences of stating that in your profile.

Ricardo: I actually took it out because I don't want to offend anybody with what I say in my profile.

Michelle: But who was telling you that you were being offensive?

Ricardo: It was a White woman, and she said, "I know that I'm not Black, but I think that you're attractive, and your views are shallow," and some other negative things about me. Well, I feel that when we go online, we go online for a purpose. Right? Then the sites ask questions, and we pretty much state what we want. Right? So how can somebody else sit there and read your profile and say, "OK, well anyway, you shouldn't be like that." I have the option when I get on here to say what the hell I want.

Michelle: Right. People say, "Because I'm not this, you're shallow. You should want me." So how did you respond in that situation?

Ricardo: I probably shouldn't have done it, but I just took all of the criteria about who I want as far as race out of my profile.

Another thing that I put on my profile—and that a lot of guys put on their profile is—"I like thick women." Thick means different things to different people. I think that it's important to be clear about what you are looking for, but you have to strike a balance and not tell too much. With body type, it's a little easier to determine whether you meet someone's criteria.

Michelle: I have taken out of my profile that I like younger men. People automatically think that means I want sex because they think, "Oh she's a cougar. So, if she's a cougar, she just wants sex." I mean, there *were* times when I was online, as I say, "for entertainment purposes only."

Ricardo: Or they're thinking that you're going to take care of their little asses.

Michelle: Yeah, be a sugar mama or whatever. But I find again that the people that respond to that are the older guys. The guys my age and older are the ones that are offended that I like younger guys.

Ricardo: But you can't get online—and that's the one thing I talk to guys about—and be political. You can't argue with everybody about their views because people have their views, and you have to understand that.

Michelle: Right. OK, so then what about interests? Do guys look to see if women have interests similar to them?

Ricardo: Yes, we do.

Michelle:	Like what? Give me some examples of the types of interests guys like to see. Are they athletic-based or …?
Ricardo:	A lot of guys love women who work out. That's cool.
Michelle:	So, for me, I like MMA. A lot of guys reach out to me because I like mixed martial arts.
Ricardo:	Really?
Michelle:	Fighting. They're like, "Wow, you like boxing and MMA?"
Ricardo:	Do you just say that because you know guys like that?
Michelle:	No, I really like those things. You know I really like those things.
Ricardo:	Yeah, that's true. I think that profiles are subjective. Women should be honest, not tell too much, and they really should probe men to see if they meet the criteria that the women state in their profile. Maybe you could leave some things out and let them unfold over time when you interact with him.

We have purposely not discussed issues of faith. Our omission is not one of disregard, but rather one of respect. We both have noted that many profiles state that the men or women are seeking "God fearing" partners or partners who share their faith. We respect that and recognize that finding someone who shares your values and religious beliefs is a very personal matter.

We also have not addressed issues related to same-sex dating. We do not have personal experience and would not want to

31

speculate in any way. We are very interested in learning more about the online experiences of people searching for same-sex relationships or companionship or fun. So if you have a story, or two, please contact us, we would love to hear from you.

Reaching out

Michelle:	So, once you've determined—based on a picture and a profile—that you'd like to learn more about a woman, what do you typically say to reach out to them for the first time?
Ricardo:	It depends on the profile. If she has a nice smile, I will typically say, "You have a very beautiful smile—keep doing it," or, "Your smile made me smile," or "I enjoyed reading your profile." I leave it open and don't say that they can contact me. I've already expressed an interest, so, if she's interested in me, we'll see where it leads.
Michelle:	Online, reaching out to someone isn't the only option you have when you're interested. A lot of the sites let you see who's viewed you. Right? So, in my case, I have this little strategy I use where if I view someone's profile and I like it, they'll know that I visited their page.
Ricardo:	Right—and you wait for a response.
Michelle:	I wait for them to reach out to me. In some cases, though, I'll reach out to them.
Ricardo:	OK, what cases are those?

Michelle: Typically if he's said something in his profile that opens the door for me to say something or gives me a chance to answer a question. I remember one guy said he was hoping to meet a woman who had the recipe for Red Lobster's biscuits so they could make them together. How could I resist reaching out to him? I remember specifically viewing your profile when we initially started to get to know each other. I viewed your profile, but I didn't message you at all. Then you messaged me. I don't know if you messaged me because you saw who had viewed you, or if you found me another way.

Ricardo: I did. I did. I messaged you because you viewed me.

Michelle: Okay, so I looked at you, but I didn't say anything. I had thoughts about you, but I didn't say anything.

Ricardo: What kind of thoughts?

Michelle: Oh boy. Yeah, I was like, "Oh he's attractive." I don't remember what you said in your profile.

Ricardo: Which shows me that you women are just as visual as we are.

Michelle: Well, we are sometimes—the visual is important. But that being said, if you're a traditional kind of guy versus a modern kind of guy, do you have any negative opinions about a woman who reaches out to you first? Do you feel like maybe she loses a little bit of the upper hand or that she gives away some of her power if she approaches you?

Ricardo: No, I don't think so. Maybe for a split second we might think that she gives away some of her power at the outset because she reached out first. We may think, "Oh, she likes me." But that doesn't last. Once the two of you get to talking, any smart person would know that that's not the case. You just happened to reach out to me before I reached out to you. I like you just as much as you like me.

Michelle: I remember one case in particular where the guy I was talking to said, "Oh yeah, I remember when I reached out to you," and I was thinking, "No, I reached out to you first." I didn't say it, of course, but it really does get to the point where you actually can forget who reached out to who because it doesn't matter. It stops being important. I think that as women, we come to expect that a man will be the aggressor online, just like in our general dating life.

One woman who has been dating online off and on for about three years said that she never reaches out to men. She only responds when guys who she's interested in reach out to her. She lamented to Michelle that she wasn't attracting the kinds of guys that she had hoped. Michelle told her that maybe she should be a little more aggressive—if she saw a guy that she liked she should initiate contact. Well, never one to do anything half-heartedly, this woman set about messaging. She sent between ten and fifteen messages initiating contact with men who she found appealing. After a month, she received her first and only reply: "Thank you for your message. I typically prefer taller women. Best of luck in your search." Needless to say, she never will again Do What Michelle Did.

Ricardo:	That's the thing. A lot of times women won't say anything because of the rules that women have, even with online dating.
Michelle:	But I think men have rules too, Ricardo.
Ricardo:	We have rules, but our rules aren't like yours. Some of you see a guy that you're immensely attracted to, but you just won't say anything because of your rule that he's supposed to reach out to you first.
Michelle:	But it's because we feel that you guys then have a negative opinion of us if we reach out first.
Ricardo:	But we're in a different time right now. Women *can* be the aggressor. What's wrong with reaching out first? If you like somebody and you happen to come across his page—maybe he hasn't seen your page yet—what's the problem with saying 'Hi?'

Speaking of rules, every person who we interviewed and to whom we spoke mentioned that they'd had sexual encounters with people they met online. In each instance, whether the interviewee was a man or a woman, they stated that by sharing intimate conversations or texts or other communications prior to meeting, some of the typical resistance to sex early in a relationship is cut shorter when a relationship begins online.

Michelle:	I think that online dating can create a false sense of security that can lead to physical involvement quicker than you would have it in a traditional setting. But I also think

that men often tip their hand about what they're really looking for online because I know that if a guy starts asking me really soon about the size of my breasts or what my bra size is—and it's been done…

Ricardo: Really? I need to tell my fellow brothers not to do that.

Michelle: No, I prefer that because then at least I know what he's about. He's too stupid to know that he's just told me that he's only interested in me for sex because at the same time he's asking about my bra size, he's saying that he's looking for a long-term relationship. His lack of finesse ends up working to my benefit.

Ricardo: Yeah, because you know what he's about. So you can get the hell away from him. Right?

Michelle: Exactly. Unless he's for entertainment purposes only.

One of the men we interviewed said that he quickly moves from electronic communication to telephonic and text communication. He has an agenda that is generally based on getting sex, so he reaches out knowing that he wants to meet the woman as soon as possible. He initiates communication or responds to women who reach out to him. They share pictures—sexting is huge in online dating, and he quickly assesses whether the women will be interested in meeting. So, for him, it's online contact, personal means of communication, flirting, sharing pictures, and then meeting. This process can transpire over the course of a few hours or a few weeks.

Chapter 3 Social Butterfly or Shut-In?

Michelle: So, in terms of deciding when to step up the communication from electronic to personal, how do you transition from written word to spoken word? To give our readers a little of our personal background, you and I met online. We exchanged maybe one or two limited messages over a week or so.

Ricardo: We really never talked on the phone.

Michelle: We talked on the phone only because that's a rule that I have.

Ricardo: Right before I came to see you.

Michelle: Correct. My rule is that I will not meet a man if we have not spoken on the phone, and that has two purposes. One is that I guess I'm a little bit of a snob when it comes to intelligence. I would like to believe that the person who wrote the profile is the same person I'm going to meet, and you can tell a lot about a person by the way that they speak to you or communicate with you verbally.

Ricardo: So what's to say that I wasn't crazy in the head? You really think that one brief conversation will let you know that a man's not crazy?

Michelle: Of course you could still be crazy, but at least you'd be a well-spoken crazy man.

Ricardo: Okay, Michelle. See, more rules.

Michelle:	Seriously, the other part is that it's a safety mechanism for me. It may not even make sense to other people, but for me, I have to have at least one phone conversation before we meet face-to-face. You and I had a brief conversation. You did that because I stated to you that it was important to me. And we met because your profile said that you were into spontaneity and that appealed to me a lot.
Ricardo:	That was my word, 'spontaneous.'
Michelle:	I will never forget that. That night when we just happened to be online at the same time, and you said, "Let's do something spontaneous! Let's meet." Then, for my safety purposes, I said, "Well, OK, let's chat just for a minute."
Ricardo:	I understood that. I understood that.
Michelle:	Right. You respected it.
Ricardo:	I called you at work.
Michelle:	Right. I didn't give you my cell number until we spoke on my work phone. I gave you my office number. I found out through an unfortunate stalking incident that you can search someone's cell number and get their home address or close to it. Anyway, I think we may have met sooner than other people do, but maybe not. You tell me about that because you're not a big phone talker and neither am I. Neither of us likes to spend hours on the phone.

Ricardo:	No, not at all.
Michelle:	So talk to me then about the typical transition for you from written word to face-to-face or phone contact. How does it work in your world?
Ricardo:	In my world, when I see somebody I like, or they see me and they like me, they might say something. So I take a look at their profile and say, "Okay. Nice. I'm interested." Then I say, "Okay, so very nice profile. How are you? What's going on today? How was your day today?" It usually goes from there to her asking, "Well, would you like to exchange numbers?" I'm not a phone talker. So I say, "Okay, yeah, we can exchange numbers." I'm not saying that I'm going to call you or anything because a lot of times I don't even call. I also ask women for their numbers, sometimes, but again, there's no guarantee that I will call.
Michelle:	Really?
Ricardo:	Yeah. But if I'm interested, I might. We exchange numbers, and I might text you. So we might start texting back and forth.

We'll pause here, because any woman reading this right now just had a moment where the needle skipped on the record. Did Ricardo just say that he asks women for their numbers but doesn't call them? Yes, he did. And not only did he admit that he does this, but so did a number of other men who we interviewed. Here's *their* "logic." When a man asks for a woman's phone number, he has every intention of calling her—at the moment that he asks for her number. However, somewhere between getting her number and actually calling, he comes across the BBD—bigger, better deal. Either he finds someone who he likes better, or he just loses focus. So there it is. We can put it to bed once and for all. It really has little to do with the woman who isn't called—it's the guy. He's decided for one reason or another not to pursue. Doesn't do much for the female ego, but it's the truth. Back to the convo…

Michelle: So your relationships stay electronic for a while?

Ricardo: Yes. I like to keep it electronic for a while. It's not that long, but I say, "Let's just text each other like we've been communicating through the site and get to know each other a little bit. Then maybe I'll feel more comfortable with actually speaking to you on the phone." After a while, women say to me, "Well, are we ever going to talk on the phone instead of texting each other?" And I say, "All right," and I call them. Usually, when I call and they hear my voice, they feel more comfortable, like, "Okay. You kind of sound like what I thought you would sound like." Then, we go from there. Usually, I'm not on the phone too long. But for me, once we start talking on the phone, I'm feeling, "Okay, so when do we meet?"

Michelle: So, once you've made verbal communication, you're ready to meet?

Every person we interviewed stated that they were online to find someone, whether for short- or long-term purposes. Everyone was interested in meeting the people face-to-face that they initially met online. So whether electronic communication lasted for days or weeks or merely hours, they each wanted to meet the people they liked. That is not the case for everyone.

Shut-in

Michelle:	What about not meeting? Have you come across women who, for whatever reason, you never meet, even though you all talk and talk and talk? What do you think is going on there? Have you asked them?
Ricardo:	I have. I think that something's not right. I think that there might be a man behind all of that who doesn't want to tell me that he's not a woman. If it goes on too long, I start thinking, "Why don't you want to meet? Either you don't look like your picture, or the picture is not you, or you're a man."
Michelle:	I've had two occasions where people have put pictures up of guys that weren't them.
Ricardo:	Really?
Michelle:	Yes. I never actually met them, but it's a hunch that I had. They would not send any other pictures of themselves. In one case, a guy said, "Why do women always ask me for more pictures?" And I thought, "Because you're not the guy in the picture, and women can sense that." Their profile pictures looked like they could have been lifted from a print ad or something, so you chat with them and go with it for a little while.

Don't Do What We Did!

Ricardo:	I had a situation where somebody was using my profile. Well, actually it was a woman who was angry with me, and she posted my picture and said I wasn't a good dude.
Michelle:	I believe it. But that's a little different than a man using your picture as his. How did you find out that she'd done that?
Ricardo:	Someone who knew me said they knew that it wasn't me. Why do people do that, though?

Out of every person we interviewed, Michelle was the only person who had not met people who had presented themselves falsely in their profile pictures. In each case, when people made arrangements to meet someone who was not the person in the profile picture, amazingly, that person would explain that he or she didn't feel that the other person would be interested in them if they had put up their own picture. What's interesting about this approach is that by doing this, they most assuredly guaranteed that they would not hear from the person who had been duped—and unanimously that is what occurred.

Another phenomenon that could fit in the "shut-in" category is the number of folks who are overseas, for work or war, who have profiles online. In some instances, they are not meeting because of obvious geographic limitations, but in many cases they are already married and just seeking pen pals.

Chapter 4 Sex, Lies and Dashed Expectations

Meeting your date's representative

"Online dating is about words," said one of our women interviewees. She recounted experiences where the men she met were not who they had initially held themselves out to be. In two cases, the men said that they were looking for long-term relationships and wives, but they were already married. She'd spent hours talking with these men. They had spent time in her home, but she had never met their friends or family. Another woman said that she met her current fiancé online about three years ago. The first time they spoke, their conversation lasted more than five hours. Prior to meeting, they spent many, many hours talking by phone. He was a truck driver, and her job enabled her to spend long hours on the phone, as well.

Michelle:	In terms of representing your true self, when can a woman begin to feel that she's meeting the real guy? You've already said that in many ways a lot of what we're hearing, especially early on, is what men think we want to hear. Men will wine and dine us because they think that's going to get them to a certain point. So at what point can we begin to believe that we're meeting the real him?
Ricardo:	Honestly, it's just a matter of time. Only time and actions over time will tell you who a person really is.

The men we spoke with all stated two things: you always receive signals when people are not who they hold themselves out to be, but many times we ignore the signals. The other thing is that having sex early on does not negatively impact the chance of a long-term relationship. Men say that the true test is whether he takes down his profile. Every man said that because of the chance of the BBD, men must take down their profiles. Otherwise, they will be tempted to continue to see other women. One man said that he'd met a woman who he really liked, then he got a message from a really attractive woman and thought, "Damn, why didn't I take my profile down?" Men also meet women who are not who they hold themselves out to be. The key is watching for consistency and congruence between actions and words. It's important to meet one another's friends and families over time and follow your instincts.

Ricardo:	You and I met at the gym, and then we sat in the grocery store and talked for hours. That shows that we might start off being interested because of physical attraction—sex, sex, sex—but if you actually meet somebody with substance, then it can work and be more—although there was some sexual tension between us.
Michelle:	There was sexual tension.
Ricardo:	You were looking at my pecs and you were digging me a little bit…
Michelle:	Maybe a little.
Ricardo:	Yeah, just a little and I was digging you, too.
Michelle:	Immensely. It was mutual. But we digress.
Ricardo:	Yeah, but we had a great conversation. The first conversation was great.
Michelle:	Right.
Ricardo:	You can always tell in the beginning when you first meet somebody if it's going to be something deep like a relationship because of the conversation and whether you feel

comfortable. If I feel comfortable, I pretty much talk your head off.

Michelle: I know. Do you really think that you speak for most men?

Ricardo: I do. I do because everybody that I've talked to tells me the same thing. Initially, what they're looking for is sex, and they will say anything and do anything to get it.

Michelle: Maybe you need better friends.

Ricardo: No, it's not about getting better friends. Even guys that I went to school with said the same thing. I've talked to a wide variety of men, in terms of race and socioeconomic status. Everyone is interested in the physical in the beginning. But, they all say that it can change and that it does change. As soon as they meet and interact with that person who they connect with on a deeper level, then it turns into something else.

Michelle: But, bottom line, we want to know when we're going to meet the real him.

Ricardo: I don't want to say after sex, but I would say, for me, I know what I'm going to do after two dates. If a guy still shows interest in you after you've had sex—and I'm not saying that you have to have sex—and he wants to do things with you outside of the bedroom, then you know he's really interested in you.

Michelle:	But a lot of guys come around until they get sex. So, I say again, at what point can we know that we've met you all?
Ricardo:	It's tough.
Michelle:	So, if *you* can't figure it out and *you* have a penis, how are we supposed to figure this out?
Ricardo:	No. I figured it out for me and then the guys I talk to…
Michelle:	Okay, so when does she know she's meeting the real you? At what point has she met the real you?
Ricardo:	The real me?
Michelle:	Yes.
Ricardo:	I would say probably not on the first date. She may be getting the extra special good treatment.
Michelle:	She gets the charming Ricardo?
Ricardo:	Yeah, but I would say that by the second date, she's getting a lot of me. By the third date and after, then it's all me.
Michelle:	When you say "date," do you mean meeting or do you mean real date?
Ricardo:	Meeting, whatever.
Michelle:	Face-to-face?
Ricardo:	Face-to-face.

Michelle:	So by the third face-to-face meeting with you, it's all you?
Ricardo:	Yeah, with *me*. Because after that I get comfortable. It takes a little while to get comfortable with anybody. I would think that's true for women, too. You're not getting the real woman in the beginning. You're getting who she thinks you want her to be.
Michelle:	But I think she's being honest typically.
Ricardo:	She might be honest about what she wants, but, in the beginning, she's not giving me attitude and all of that.

The reality is that this was one of Michelle and Ricardo's most difficult and contentious conversations. Knowing when someone has shown you who they really are is one of the most difficult parts of any romantic relationship. We really don't have any good answers here, other than take your time getting to know someone. We make no judgments or hard and fast rules when it comes to making the decision to be physical in your relationship. The best advice we can give is to trust your own best judgment and follow your inner voice.

Safety matters

We've touched upon some safety issues, with regard to profile pictures of your children, home, car, and belongings. Posting pictures of your home, your cars, your jewelry (yes, people do it), or other material possessions are just invitations to be robbed. One of the men we spoke with mentioned that he let a woman come to his home for a sexual encounter and she stole his watch.

Ricardo:

I actually prefer to just meet a woman without a whole lot of communication. There are those times, like I said earlier, that I'll text with her, and we may talk once, but I really just prefer to meet.

Michelle:

But that's because you're looking for sex.

Ricardo:

The thing is, I will meet without speaking on the phone. I'm like, "Let's just meet. We can just see each other."

Michelle:

I remember when you said that to me. I remember. I was like, "No."

Ricardo:

See, a lot of women like you have those rules like, "I need to talk to this man on the phone." So we'll talk. Cool. You talked to me, and you think I have a little bit of intelligence, and I sound like a nice guy—which is still crazy because that doesn't mean that I'm not a bad person. We've already discussed that I can tell you anything. To protect yourself you must ensure that a guy can give you all the instruments you need to know to ensure that you're comfortable around him. I can give you my first and last name. If I can't give you my first and last name, something's wrong. Right?

Michelle:

Right.

Ricardo:

You can Google my name. We're in the information technology age. You can Google somebody and you can pretty much figure out what's going on with them. So, if we meet, you pretty much know who I am.

Michelle: There are some things I do for safety's sake. I definitely meet in a public place. If we are going to be riding somewhere, I either take a picture of or text message your license plate number to my sister, Maya. She's always my safety.

Ricardo: Yeah, you did that to me, huh? Because you let me drive you a few blocks from the gym to the Safeway where we sat and had our first "date."

Michelle: I did that to you. I texted your license plate number to Maya.

Ricardo: I didn't realize that you did it.

Michelle: It wasn't something for you to know. And sometimes I'll take a picture of the car and/or license plate and text it to Maya.

Ricardo: It's like, "Click." Take the picture huh?

Michelle: Exactly. I introduced you to my trainer at the gym so that at least one other person had your name and face. Sometimes, my friends and I exchange the phone numbers of the men we're meeting. I'll text her the person's name and phone number. She does the same with me. "This is where we're meeting. This is what time we're meeting. I should be calling you within an hour or two. If you don't hear from me, text me or something." Because it is the information age. Do you think that men take similar precautions? Should they have any similar safety concerns that women do, or is that pretty much our area?

Ricardo:	I would think more so for women. Men have safety issues, but I really can't see a man feeling physically threatened by a woman, for the most part. I can see maybe between a man and a man.

One of our male interviewees, the one whose watch was lifted from his home, also had an altercation early in his online dating experience. He was bringing a girl back to her home, and, as he was dropping her off, a guy approached the car and tried to rob him at gunpoint. He was still in the car, so he pulled off. He never interacted with the woman again, and, to this day, he really believes that she set him up.

Ricardo:	I think men really have to worry about the women who are out to try to get their money, scam them, and stalk them.
Michelle:	Yeah, stalkers.
Ricardo:	We talked earlier about situations where people were not the people in their profile pictures. That could really be dangerous because you're meeting someone who isn't who he or she says. You don't even have a true picture. Why do people do that?
Michelle:	I don't know. I would say in terms of safety and stalkers, even women have to worry about women because some of those people that you don't actually meet face-to-face could be hiding that they're married or in a long-term relationship. I had a situation where I exchanged one e-mail with a guy, and he was apparently in a long-term relationship. She wreaked havoc in my life.

Ricardo: Really?

Michelle: She Googled me, found me, and started calling and e-mailing me. She put a personal ad on craigslist saying that I was looking for sex. I found that out because a guy called my cell phone and was like, "Oh, I got your number off of craigslist." I said, "I'm not selling anything." He said, "No, in the personal ads." I had to report it. The craigslist people had to get involved. It was crazy. I'd never met the man and she went through all of that. It was awful for me.

Ricardo: See, that's the thing you deal with when you're online because you kind of open yourself up to a lot of crazy situations. Women probably deal with it more so than we do, but we do deal with it.

One male interviewee stated that online dating had made him a better judge of character. In his words, "Online dating has sharpened my B.S. detector, and I think it has for many women too."

Like we said in the section about meeting your date's representative, ask yourself some questions and make some observations when interacting with someone. Is the person following through on their promises? Are they calling when they said they would? Or does it seem that they are just saying what you want to hear to get to the next level? Your answers to these questions over time should help you.

As Ricardo said, we're in the information age. One of the women we interviewed had an inkling that something was off with one of the men she was dating, so, while he was visiting her, she had her cousin take information from his car. Using his VIN and license plate number, she was able to find out that he was married, that the car was registered to his wife, and that the name he was using was actually his son's name. When she threatened to tell his wife if he didn't shut down his profile, he shut it down … and opened an account on another site. She found out because he gave her cousin the same story, and, when they looked at the picture, it was him!

A male interviewee mentioned the addictive nature of online dating. There appears to be an endless supply of new men and women to interact with for whatever purposes you choose. This can make it unsafe for the uninitiated or the naïve who don't realize that there are people online who have been on and off for years and who, in some cases, have no intention of having a relationship. Typically, those people are in other relationships and are using online dating as an avenue for infidelity. In fact, one woman stated, "He was home with his wife when we had most of our communications online." She also stated that if she were single now (she's married to a man she met through a mutual friend), she would not date online.

She and women she knows have met men who were not the men in the pictures on the profile. They have met men at homes that were not their actual residences but were apartments they rented for sexual encounters. Finally, two women met men at what was supposed to be their homes and found themselves in houses that had only beds and no other furniture.

Given recent news about sexual assaults by men that women met online, we say please heed the warning signs and do not allow "words" to cloud your judgment when it comes to your safety.

Sex matters

Hands down, sex is something that everyone talks about with respect to online dating. One website that is strictly about hooking up for sex earned over $250 million last year. That being said, in almost every profile on the sites that are not expressly set up for sex, people state that they are either looking for a relationship or are open to having a relationship. Men state that while they are typically not "looking" for a relationship, the reality is that if they meet a woman who "grows" on them, they will willingly have a relationship with her. One guy we interviewed summed it up this way: "I'm amazed that men and women are on the same sheet of music but take different approaches to arrive at that point." In other words, men say that women set out looking for a relationship and screen all interactions based on whether the man will be a good mate. Men are generally looking for sex, and, if they come across a woman who seems like she would make a good mate, they are open to having a monogamous relationship.

Ricardo: What's funny is that people say they don't want to rush things, and, "Let's take our time," but as soon as you get together, all that goes out the window.

Michelle: Well, that leads to that statistic that we saw that stated that somewhere between 30 and 53 percent of women say that they have sex on a first online date.

Ricardo: Why do you think that is?

Michelle: I think that it's because in typical circumstances you have all of these hours of attention and midnight phone calls and sexy text messages—or maybe not even sexy text messages—text messages just saying, "Hey I'm thinking about you. You crossed my mind." Now, he could be sending that as a mass text to a bunch of women. Who knows?

Ricardo: This is before you actually meet, right?

Michelle: This is before you actually meet where you're sharing...

Ricardo: You're building something, right?

Michelle: Exactly. You have built all of this intimacy or perceived intimacy between you so that by the time you meet, shoot, some people make their first date at a hotel on purpose so they can have sex. And these are people who say that they are looking for a long-term relationship.

Ricardo: So if you meet that person and that person looks like their picture, looks good to you in person, it's very easy to just jump right out the window, so to speak, and just do...you know...

Michelle: What comes naturally between grown folks.

Ricardo: Yeah, what grown people do.

Michelle: So, in terms of that, we've been taught that if a woman has sex too early— typically before ninety days—

Ricardo: Ninety days?

Michelle: Ninety days.

Ricardo: Is that what you guys are taught?

Michelle: That's what we're taught.

Ricardo: Three months?

Michelle: Yes, Ricardo. Three months. We're supposed to wait three months before we have sex with you.

Ricardo: Wow.

Michelle: Yes. You would dry up.

Ricardo: Yeah. I would probably—

Michelle: Sleep with someone else.

Ricardo: Pretty much.

Michelle: Which is what we also do during those ninety days. For women, we sleep with the guy we don't see having potential as a long-term mate, and wait to have sex with the guy who we hope will be HIM.

Ricardo: See, that's the thing. There are guys that have waited the ninety days, and she's sleeping with someone who she doesn't like as much. That's crazy.

Michelle: So let's say a woman has sex with you on your first meeting, and, in her mind, you actually have intimacy. For her, this really isn't a first date; the meeting is more like a formality because you already *know* each other. Now, let's say that you think that good girls don't have sex that soon. How do you make all of that come into alignment for a woman who is hoping that she's with the guy of her dreams? Does having sex during the first physical meeting play any role in what he may think about her?

Ricardo: You know what? I think we know immediately if it's going to be just sex, or if it's going to be more. So, a lot of times, you can sleep with somebody the first night and not hurt your chance at a relationship. If they truly like you and truly want to get to know you, it doesn't matter. *I* don't think it matters. And a lot of guys I know don't think it matters. I know a lot of guys who have met women online and slept with them rather quickly, but they're still in relationships.

Now, if you're paying close attention, Ricardo has said that he knows—and that most men know—immediately whether a relationship is going to be about just sex. But he's also said that, over time, a relationship that started off as a sexual relationship can develop into more. Here we have another conundrum. I don't know that we can give a better answer than to say that people vibe with one another, and that through communication, consistent interaction, and mutual honesty a relationship can and may develop.

We really do wish that we had a better answer, but because we're not in a relationship, we can only tell you what not to do. Don't overanalyze every interaction. Don't ignore those gut feelings that things are out of alignment. Don't use sex to try to keep someone, whether by having more than you feel comfortable having or by withholding it as a means of manipulation. Bottom line: DON'T stress, but DO heed your inner voice.

Chapter 5 Grown Folks' Business

Throughout the book we've attempted to use our own relationship, or lack thereof, and the experiences of others to show that success online is possible if you are clear about your motivations and if you are able to clearly define what 'success' means to you.

One of the women we interviewed who is now engaged to a man she met online did not even create her own profile. Her cousin created a profile for her on a website that is used for dating and playing games. Her fiancé reached out to her, and she was very clear that she had no motivation for going online because she wasn't online by choice. That being said, once she started talking with different men, she realized that there was a possibility that she would find love online.

Recently divorced, after more than ten years of marriage and three children, another woman, who would never date online again now, said that when she first got online, she was like, "Wow, a smorgasbord of men are on here." Michelle and Ricardo agreed wholeheartedly about how plentiful the sea of prospects appears, especially when you are looking for sex. During an early relationship, Michelle recalled wondering if online dating had become to sex what Amazon had become to books—punch in a few keywords, find some options, make a choice, and proceed to checkout.

Our amazing editor, Sharon, met her husband online and says that she is so happy that she bent her "rule" of not dating men whose status was "separated" because her husband-to-be was looking for a long-term relationship, and, after they met, he did get divorced. They are now quite happily married.

Ricardo and Michelle consider ourselves successful because although we were not able to make a romantic relationship work with each other, over time we have built a friendship that is based on a foundation of mutual interests and caring for one another.

   While Ricardo and Michelle are still looking for that true love we each believe exists, and are back on the site where we met, we do know for sure that if you seek long-term love, you can find it—if you Don't Do What We Did! And what, you ask, is it that we did? We seem perfect for each other after reading this book, right? Well, we failed to be honest with ourselves and, by extension, with one another. Ricardo really wasn't ready for a relationship, and Michelle had reached a point where she actually was ready for a relationship but was afraid to let down her guard. In the end, creating this book and sharing with you what goes on in the wide world of online dating, as well as how you can be successful in that world was worth the whirlwind romance and ensuing heartbreak that ~~Ricardo, Michelle~~, we experienced.

Michelle Y. Talbert & Ricardo Kingsbury

Acknowledgments

From Ricardo:

First, I would like to give thanks to God for giving me the strength, courage, and wisdom to write this book. I would like to thank my mom for raising me well and teaching me valuable lessons that I've carried with me throughout my life. Mr. and Mrs. Walker, Houseparents at Milton Hershey School, who played a big role in raising me. My Milton Hershey family for all of your comments to questions I posted while doing research. My family members and friends for your stories and input. Michelle Y. Talbert who gave me the opportunity to co-author this book. You are a great writer and a great friend....To my little brother Ricom, RIP love you and wish you were here to share this with me....

From Michelle:

I have been humbled and overwhelmed by the outpouring of love and support that I've received throughout my life, and as I embarked upon this project. I must thank my mom, Yvonne, dad, Arun, sister, Maya, grandmother, Barbara Talbert, cousins, Ja, Sakina, Monique, and Joseph Alexander Bowe, and my amazing children, Jasmine, Javier and Aaron for loving me and cheering me on through every far-fetched goal that I've ever set for myself. This book would not have been possible without the courage and support of Ricardo Kingsbury. I grew because we took this journey. Can't wait to see where it leads. Aviva Goldfarb, Julie Isaac, my Furious Flowers sisters—Sadeqa Johnson, Janae Galyn, Nicole Dennis, Cheryl Head and Diana Veiga—and our Master Teacher, Marita Golden, Clyde McElvene, The Hurston/Wright Foundation, Giovanni Turner and so many others in my writing circle, I thank you so much for your honesty and your talent. I also thank one Fly Black Chick—Yesha Callahan—for a banging website. My brother, Eric Johnson-Gamez, who never asks "why?" just says, "I'm here for you." If I did not list you by name, please know that it is an oversight of the brain and not the heart. There have been so many who have done things large and small. No act has gone unnoticed. Thank you.

From us:

We both wish to thank our editor, Sharon Honeycutt who took "our baby" and nurtured it like her own, Manjari Henderson for a cover that surpassed our wildest expectations and Al Wilson for taking a crazy idea and making a work of art, and Paul Coates and Natalie Stokes of Black Classic Press for helping us get it done! We thank each and every person who shared a story or more with us and allowed us to probe into places where many are not permitted.

About the Authors

Ricardo Kingsbury has dated online off and on since the early 2000s. He has helped men create profiles and has swapped many war stories from the trenches. He's been married twice yet still believes in true love. He believes that his online dating history needs to be shared with women. He jumped at the chance to co-author this book with Michelle. His goal is to share with women some of the do's and don'ts of online dating to make them more tactical online daters. Ricardo graduated from Milton Hershey and joined the DC Fire Department in 1991. He began his acting and modeling career in 2004. He's been in numerous commercials, TV shows, and feature films. He lives in the Washington, DC area with his daughters.

Michelle Y. Talbert married her first husband at 19 and her second at 34. She began online dating in the early 2000s and then resumed online dating after separating from her second husband in 2009. What a world of difference! As a single mom of two children, Michelle graduated from Cornell University at the age of 30 and went on to Penn Law School, receiving her law degree at 33. She is currently working on her first novel, *Divorce Party*. Michelle works and dates in Washington, DC, where she lives with her children, when they're home from college and other life activities.

For free guides and other information visit us at:

http://dontdowhatwedid.com

www.ingramcontent.com/pod-product-compliance
Lightning Source LLC
La Vergne TN
LVHW052312060326
832902LV00021B/3847